First Lessons Viola

by Katherine Curatolo

Audio Contents

1	Example 1–1	33	C Major Scale
2	Example 1–2	34	Finale from Symphony No. 1
3	Example 1–3	35	Simple Gifts
4	Example 1–4	36	Minuet
5	Example 2–1	37	Lullaby
6	Example 2–2	38	Three at a Time
7	Hot Cross Buns	39	Sonatina
8	Mary Had a Little Lamb	40	F Major Scale
9	D Major Scale	41	Londonderry Air
10	Example 3–1	42	The Thunderer
11	Twinkle, Twinkle Little Star	43	The Skater's Waltz
12	London Bridge	44	Example 16–1
13	Example 4–1	45	Autumn
14	Row, Row, Row Your Boat	46	The Irish Washerwoman
15	Can Can	47	Planxty Irwin
16	Example 5–1	48	Theme from American Quartet
17	G Major Scale	49	Silent Night
18	Frere Jacques	50	Example 19–1
19	Lightly Row	51	Example 19–2
20	Example 6–1	52	Finale from London Symphony
21	Example 6–2	53	Trumpet Voluntary
22	Have a Rest	54	Light Cavalry Overture
23	Example 7–1	55	Sleepers Awake
24	Short and Sweet	56	Minuet
25	Oh! Susanna	57	Fisher's Hornpipe
26	Example 8–1	58	Yankee Doodle
27	Smooth Sailing	59	The British Grenadiers
28	Swing Low Sweet Chariot	60	On the Bridge of Avignon
29	Ode to Joy	61	Scotland the Brave
30	Theme from New World	62	Sheep May Safely Graze
31	Example 10–1	63	Sleeping Beauty Waltz
32	Down Low	64	Intermezzo

1 2 3 4 5 6 7 8 9 0

Visit us on the Web at www.melbay.com — E-mail us at email@melbay.com

Introduction

This book serves as an introduction to playing the viola, with emphasis both on technical development and basic music reading skills. Each of the 26 lessons introduces a new concept and reinforces it through exercises and a variety of musical examples including familiar songs and classical pieces. The lessons progress from the basics of how to hold the viola to playing music incorporating multiple techniques. The included audio CD contains all exercises and pieces from the book.

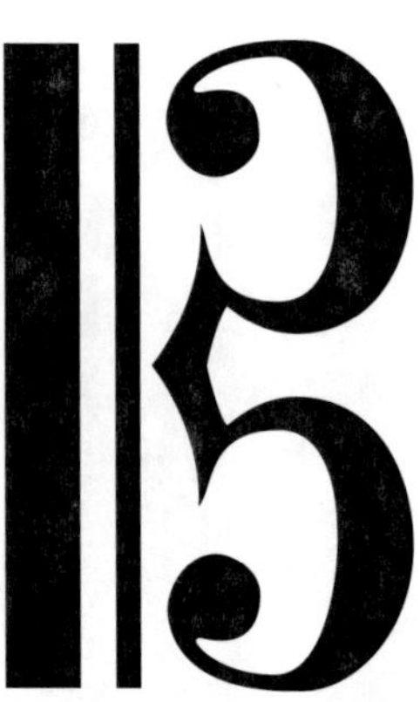

Contents

Basic Music Reading and Terminology

Music is written on a staff, which has five lines and four spaces. Viola music is written in the alto clef.

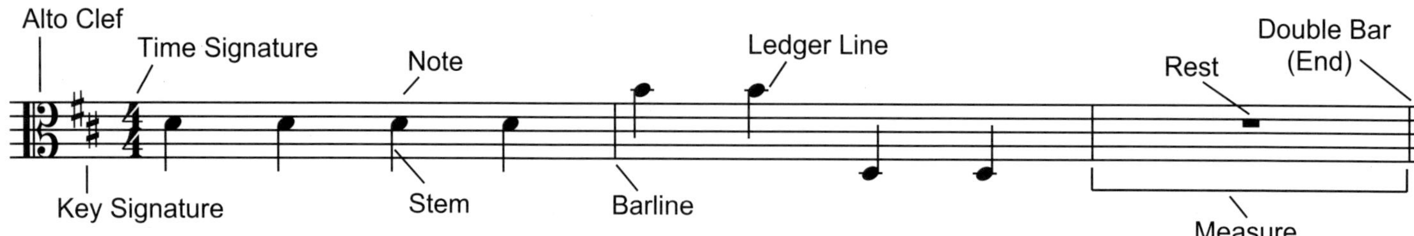

The key signature indicates whether certain notes in the key are played as a sharp (♯) or flat (♭). A sharp raises the pitch of a note, and a flat lowers the pitch. Notes that are not sharp or flat are natural, and either have no symbol or a natural sign (♮).

The time signature indicates how to count. The bottom number represents the type of note being counted, and the top number represents the number of those notes in the measure. In 4/4 time, also known as common time, the time is counted in quarter notes and there are four quarter notes in a measure. One beat equals one quarter note.

Notes in the Alto Clef:

A quarter note equals one beat, a half note equals two beats, and a whole note equals four beats.
4 quarter notes = 2 half notes = 1 whole note

The Viola and Bow

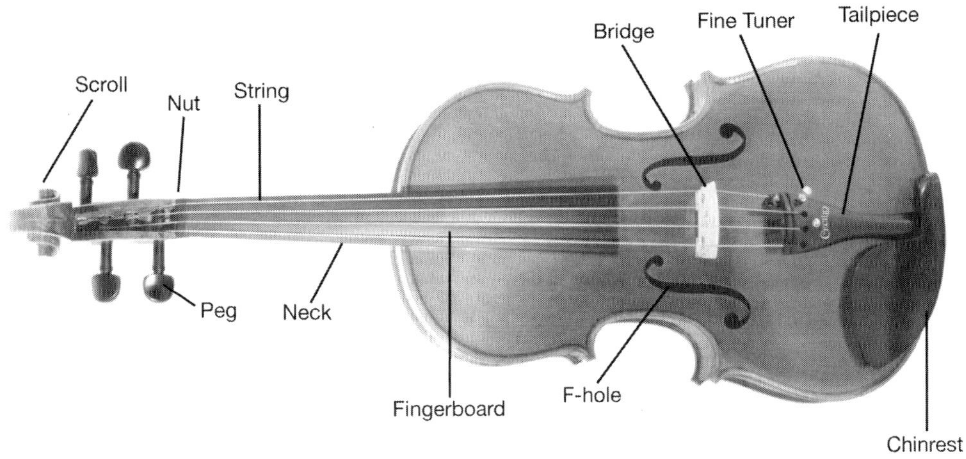

Most student instruments are equipped with fine tuners. Adjust the pitch of each string by turning the fine tuner clockwise for the pitch to go up and counterclockwise to go down. Use a tuner or match the sound of the string by ear to a tone or piano. Fine tuners will suffice unless the instrument becomes very out of tune, in which case tuning must be done with pegs. Learning to successfully use the tuning pegs takes practice. To raise the pitch using the peg, turn the peg upwards, or away from you, while gently pressing it inwards. To lower the pitch, turn the peg downwards. Avoid touching the strings in the area between the bridge and the fingerboard; finger oils will make it difficult for the bow to grip the string.

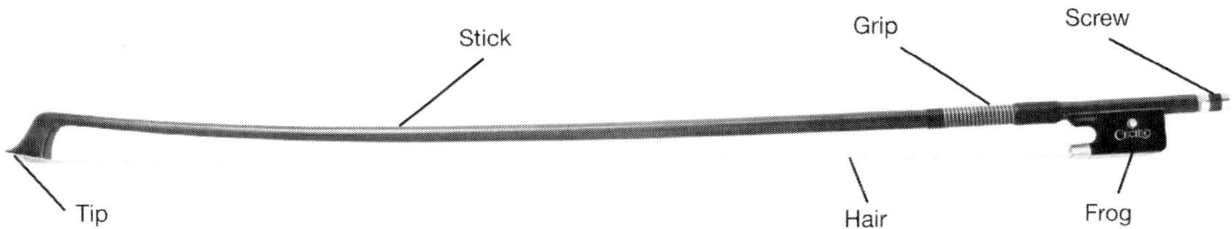

When ready to play, tighten the bow hair by turning the screw several times counterclockwise, or to the right, when the bow is held vertically. The hair is tight enough when there is a space about the size of one finger between the stick and the hair at the center of the bow. There should be a slight curve in the stick. Apply rosin to the bow for friction by gliding the full length of the bow over the rosin several times. An appropriate amount of rosin will leave a small amount of white residue on the strings. When finished playing, clean this residue from the strings and instrument with a cloth. Avoid touching the hair to keep it clean. When the bow is stored in the case, release the tension of the hair by "loosening" the bow, or turning the screw clockwise when the bow is held vertically. A few turns will be sufficient.

The viola should ideally be kept in an environment of 40 to 60% humidity, away from extreme cold or heat, out of direct sunlight and away from heaters or air conditioners. It should not be stored in a car.

Lesson 1

Holding the Viola

The goal in holding the viola and bow is to achieve a relaxed and tension–free position. There should be no gripping or squeezing. Begin by standing with feet shoulder width apart and the left foot placed slightly forward. The instrument should be balanced primarily on the shoulder with the left hand as a support. The left shoulder should not be raised and the head should remain in a neutral position, not clamped down on the chin rest or twisted to the side. Many people use a shoulder rest or pad to help support the viola. There are many different chinrest and shoulder support options, and it is best to try several in order to find the most comfortable fit.

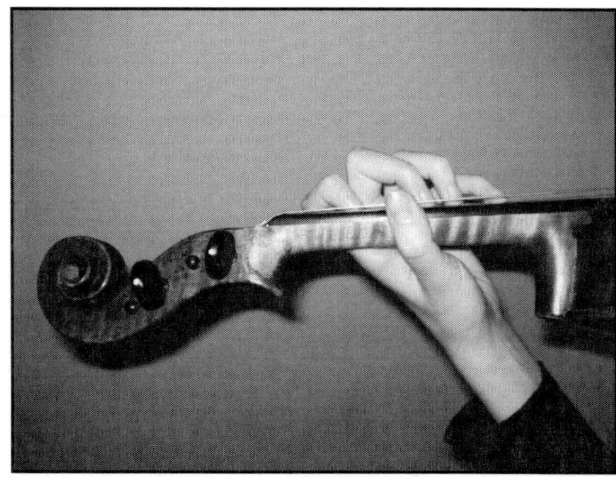

The neck of the viola should rest between the base knuckle of the index finger and the crook of the thumb, which should curve around the neck. The wrist should remain in a neutral position; it should not bend backwards or collapse inwards towards the neck. The left elbow should remain comfortably under the viola; when playing on the lower strings it will rotate slightly to the right.

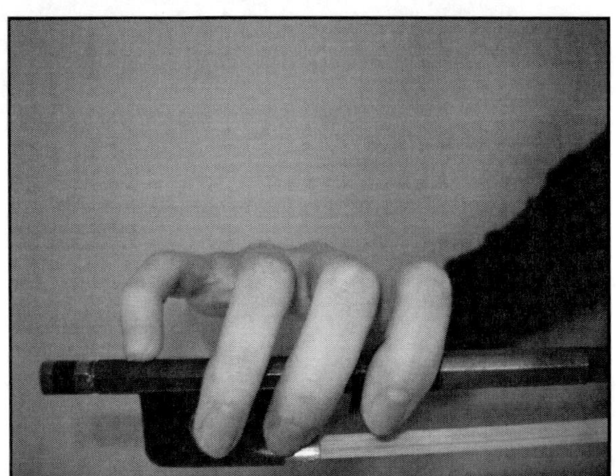

It takes time to develop a comfortable bow hold. Hold the bow near the frog with the stick touching the index finger between the middle and upper joints, the middle and ring fingers curved around the stick, and the little finger resting on the top of the stick. The thumb rests on the underside of the stick opposite the middle finger, with all joints in a curved position. The wrist should remain in a neutral position, with the upper arm held away from the body and the elbow at the same level as or slightly lower than the wrist. The right shoulder should remain relaxed and not lifted. When playing, place the bow about midway between the bridge and the fingerboard. Pull the bow in a straight line by opening the arm from the elbow, and allow the natural weight of the arm to produce a sound without pressing.

With the photos on this page as a guide, use a mirror to check for good posture and placement.

Open Strings

Strings played without putting down fingers are called **open strings**. The strings of the viola are, from lowest to highest, C, G, D, A.

"**Down bow**" means to move the bow downwards to the right. "**Up bow**" means to move the bow upwards to the left. They are shown by the following symbols:

Down bow (⊓) Up bow (V)

Practice the following exercises with the goal of producing a smooth, clear tone.

Example 1-1

Track 1

Example 1-2

Track 2

Example 1-3

Track 3

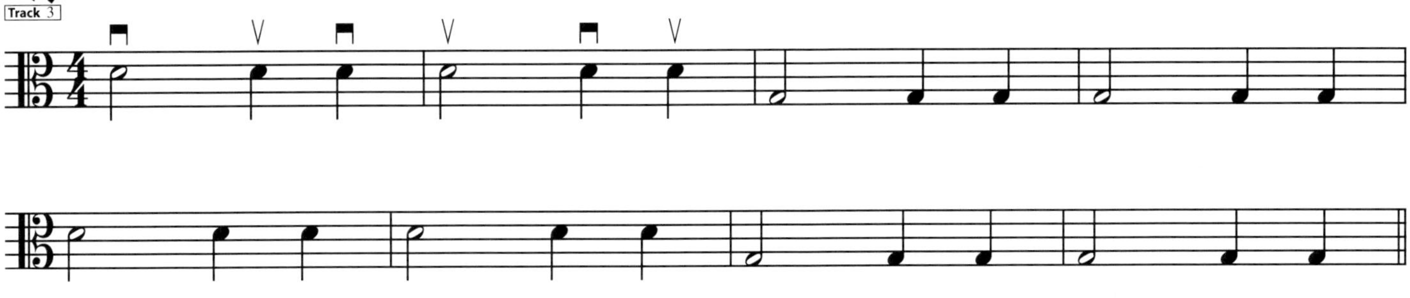

Example 1-4

Track 4

Lesson 2

First and Second Fingers on the D and A strings

The fingers on the left hand are assigned numbers 1 through 4. The index finger is 1 and the little finger is 4; the thumb does not have a number. Use the fleshy part of the fingertip to press down the string. There will be a space between the first and second fingers.

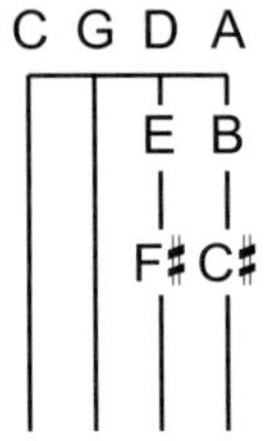

C G D A
E B
F♯ C♯

D E F♯ A B C♯

Example 2-1

Track 5

0 1 2 0

0 1 2 0

Example 2-2

Track 6

Hot Cross Buns

Track 7

Traditional

The symbol ’ means to “retake.” Lift the bow and replace it on the string for the next note.

Mary Had a Little Lamb

Track 8

Traditional

Lesson 3

D Major and Third Finger on the D and A Strings

The key of **D Major** has an F sharp and a C sharp. Place the third finger right next to the second finger, without a space.

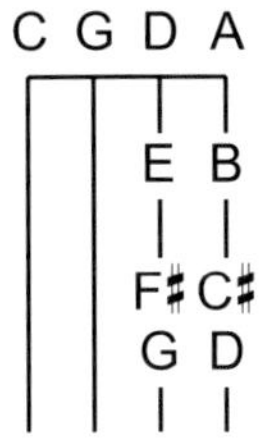

C G D A
E B
F♯ C♯
G D

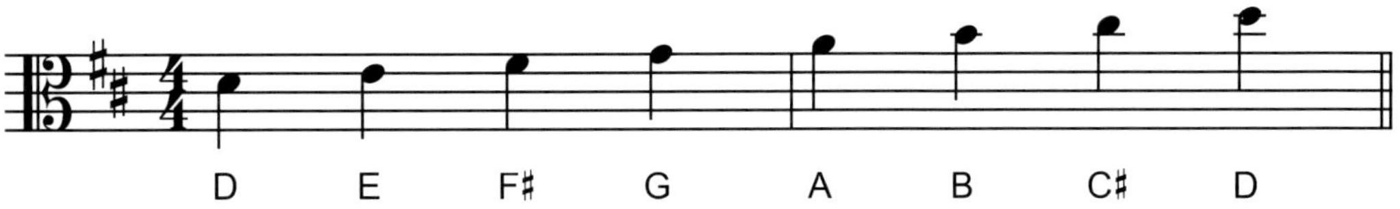

D E F♯ G A B C♯ D

D Major Scale

Track 9

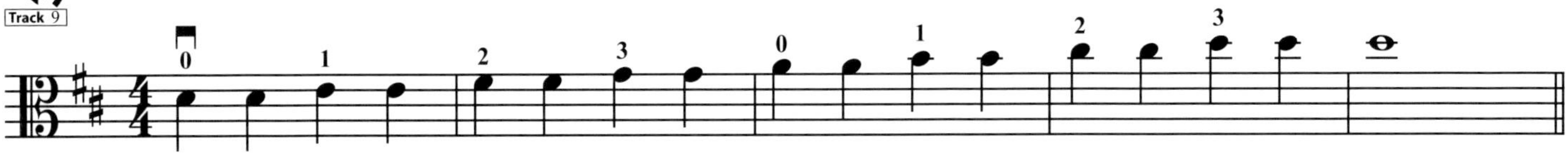

0 1 2 3 0 1 2 3

Example 3-1

Track 10

Twinkle, Twinkle Little Star

Track 11

Traditional

A **dotted half note** is worth one and a half half-notes, or three beats.

London Bridge

Track 12

Traditional

Lesson 4

Eighth Notes

An **eighth note** is worth half of a beat, and two eighth notes equal one quarter note. A single eighth note has one flag, and multiple eighth notes often are connected by a line.

Lesson 5

The G String and G Major

The key of **G major** has one sharp, F♯. The note C is natural; on the G string it is played with the third finger directly next to the second finger. On the A string, the C natural is played with a lowered second finger placed directly next to the first finger.

Lesson 6

Rests

A **rest** is a symbol that indicates a period of silence in music. Each type of note has a corresponding rest worth the same amount of time.

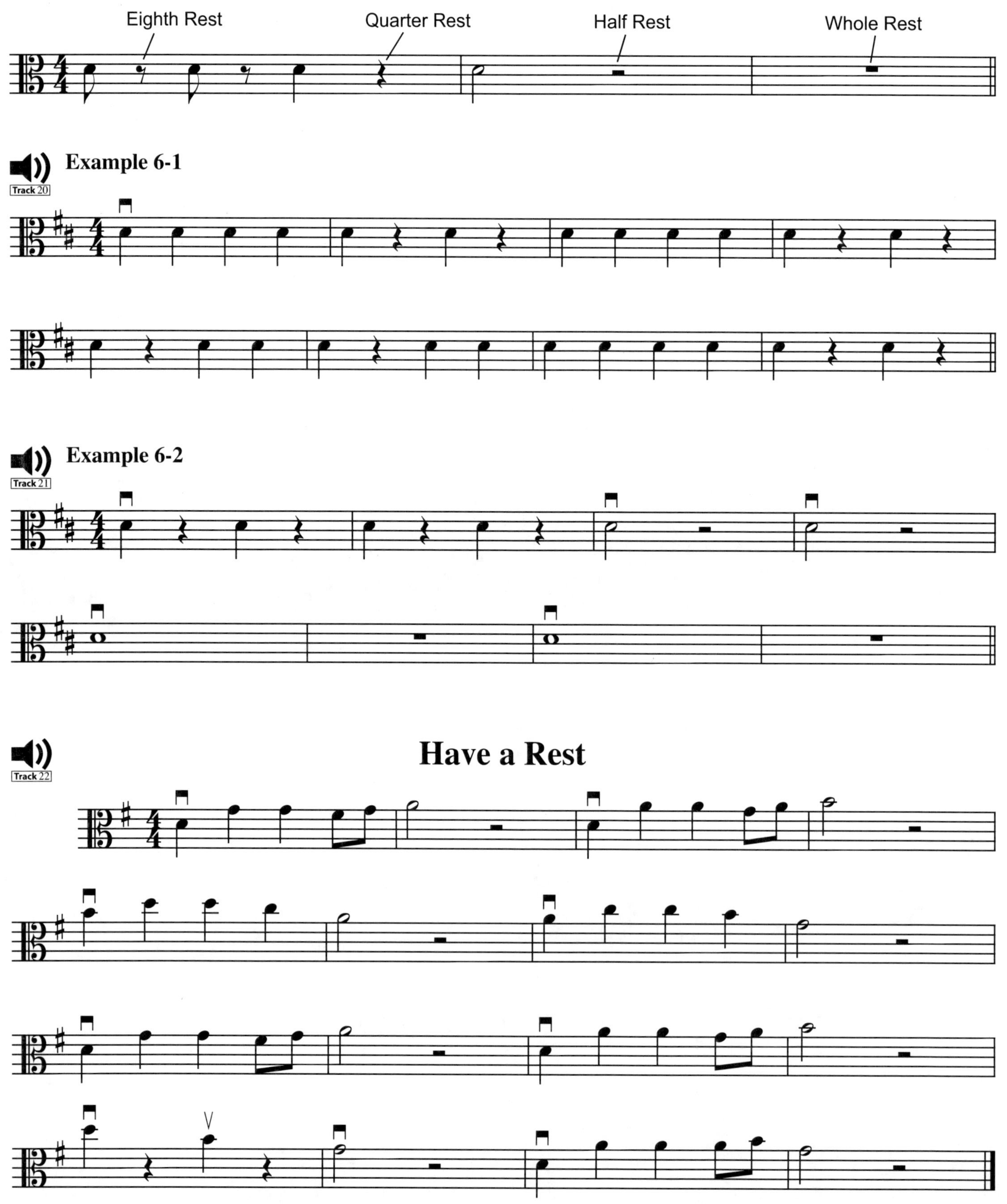

Lesson 7

Staccato

Staccato means to play in a short and detached way and is indicated by a dot above or below a note. Stop the bow on the string for a space after each note.

Lesson 8

Legato

Legato means to play in a smooth and lengthened way. Keep the bow moving to connect each note to the next without breaks.

Lesson 9

Slurs

A **slur** is a curved line over several notes that means to play all of the included notes in the same bow.

Lesson 10

The C String and C Major

The key of **C Major** has no sharps or flats. On the C string, the F natural is played with the third finger directly next to the second finger E. On the D string, the F natural is played with a lowered second finger directly next to the first finger E.

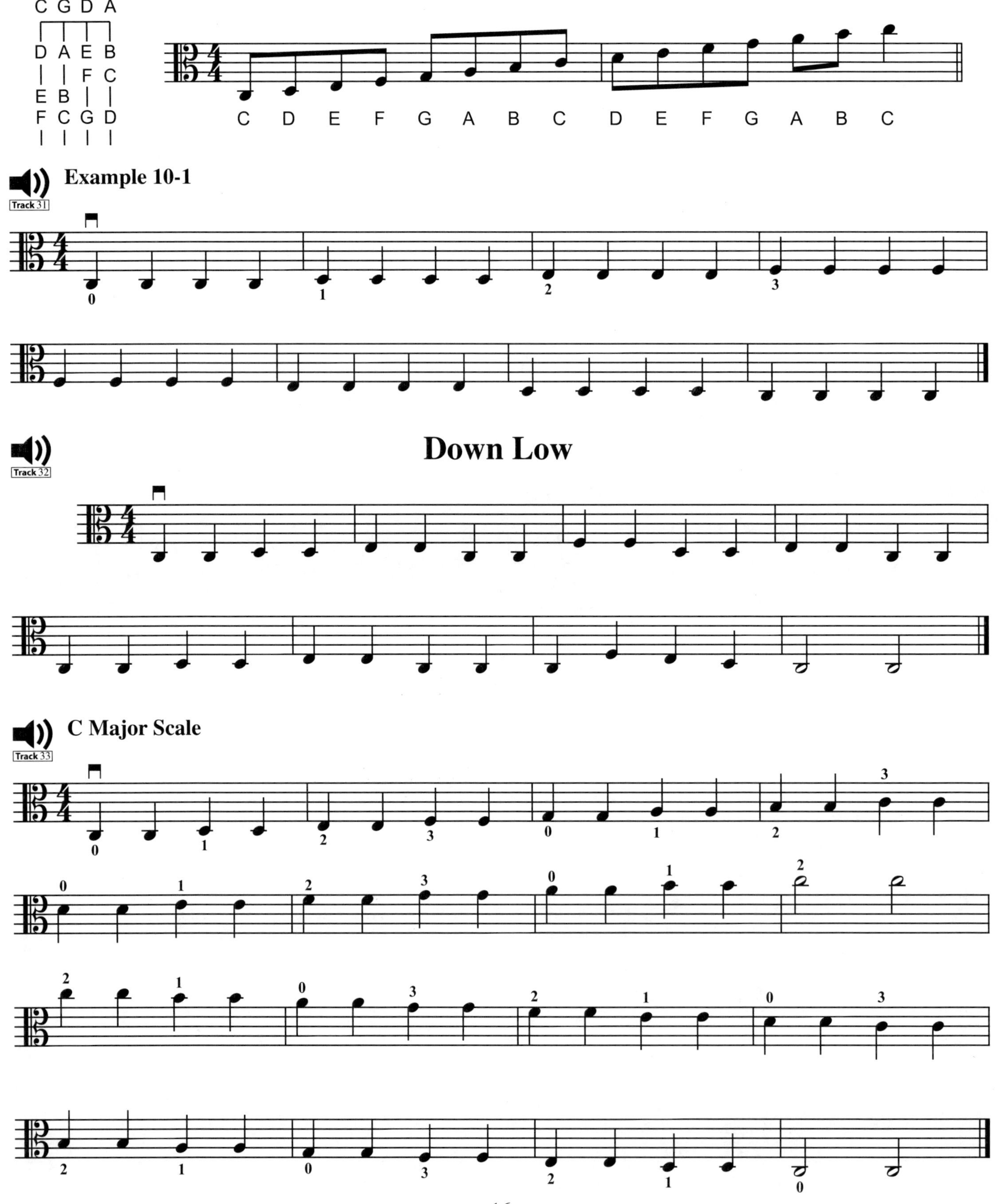

Lesson 11

Upbeats and Ties

An **upbeat**, also called a pickup, is one or more notes that occur before the first full measure of a piece. It is helpful to count silently the measure containing the upbeat before playing. A **tie** is a slur that connects two notes of the same pitch, often across a bar line.

Lesson 12

3/4 Time

In **3/4 time**, there are three beats in a measure and each beat is equal to one quarter note.

Lesson 13

Triplets and 2/4 Time

A **triplet** is a group of three notes played evenly in the space of two of the same kind of note. It is written as three notes marked with the number 3 and sometimes connected by a bracket. In 4/4 time, an eighth note triplet is played in the same amount of time as two eighth notes, or one quarter note.

Track 38

Three at a Time

In **2/4 time**, there are two beats in a measure and each beat is equal to one quarter note.

Track 39

Sonatina

William Duncombe

Lesson 14

F Major

The key of **F Major** has one flat. The B♭ is played as a lowered second finger on the G string, directly next to the first finger A natural. On the A string, the B♭ is a lowered first finger, extended backwards towards the nut.

Lesson 15

Repeat Signs

A **repeat sign** is a double bar with two dots before it. It means to return to the beginning of the piece or to the most recent repeat sign and play that section of music again.

Lesson 16

Dynamics

Dynamics is a term that describes how loudly or softly music should be played. These are the most common dynamic markings found in music:

ff - *fortissimo*, very loud   ***f*** - *forte*, loud   ***mf*** - *mezzo–forte*, medium–loud
mp - *mezzo–piano*, medium–soft   ***p*** - *piano*, soft   ***pp*** - *pianissimo*, very soft

Crescendo means to gradually become louder and can also be shown by the abbreviation cresc. or the symbol (<). *Decrescendo* means to gradually become softer and can also be shown by the abbreviation decresc. or the symbol (>).

To play more loudly, move the bow closer to the bridge and apply more pressure with the right arm and hand. To play more softly, move the bow closer to the fingerboard and use less pressure.

Example 16-1

Lesson 17

6/8 Time

In **6/8 time**, there are six beats in a measure and each beat equals one eighth note.

Track 46

The Irish Washerwoman

Traditional Irish

In G Major, the third finger on the C string is placed high, with a space between the second and third fingers. This note is F♯.

Track 47

Planxty Irwin

Turlough O'Carolan

Lesson 18

Dotted Quarter Notes

A **dotted quarter note** is worth one and a half quarter notes, or three eighth notes. It is written as a quarter note with a dot next to it. Similarly, a dotted quarter rest is written as a quarter note rest with a dot next to it.

Lesson 19

Fourth Finger

The **fourth finger** plays the same note as the next highest open string. The fourth finger on the C string is G, on the G string is D, and on the D string is A. Generally, we choose between the fourth finger and the open string in order to minimize string crossings. In the keys introduced so far, the fourth finger on the A string is E natural. When the third finger is a natural note, there will be a space between the third and fourth fingers. When the third finger is a sharp note, the fourth finger will be placed directly next to the third.

Lesson 20

Accidentals

An **accidental** is a note that is not included in a certain key signature. It is indicated by a sharp (♯), flat (♭), or natural (♮) sign. An accidental remains in effect for one measure unless marked otherwise. A G♯ on the D string is played with a high third finger.

Trumpet Voluntary

Jeremiah Clarke

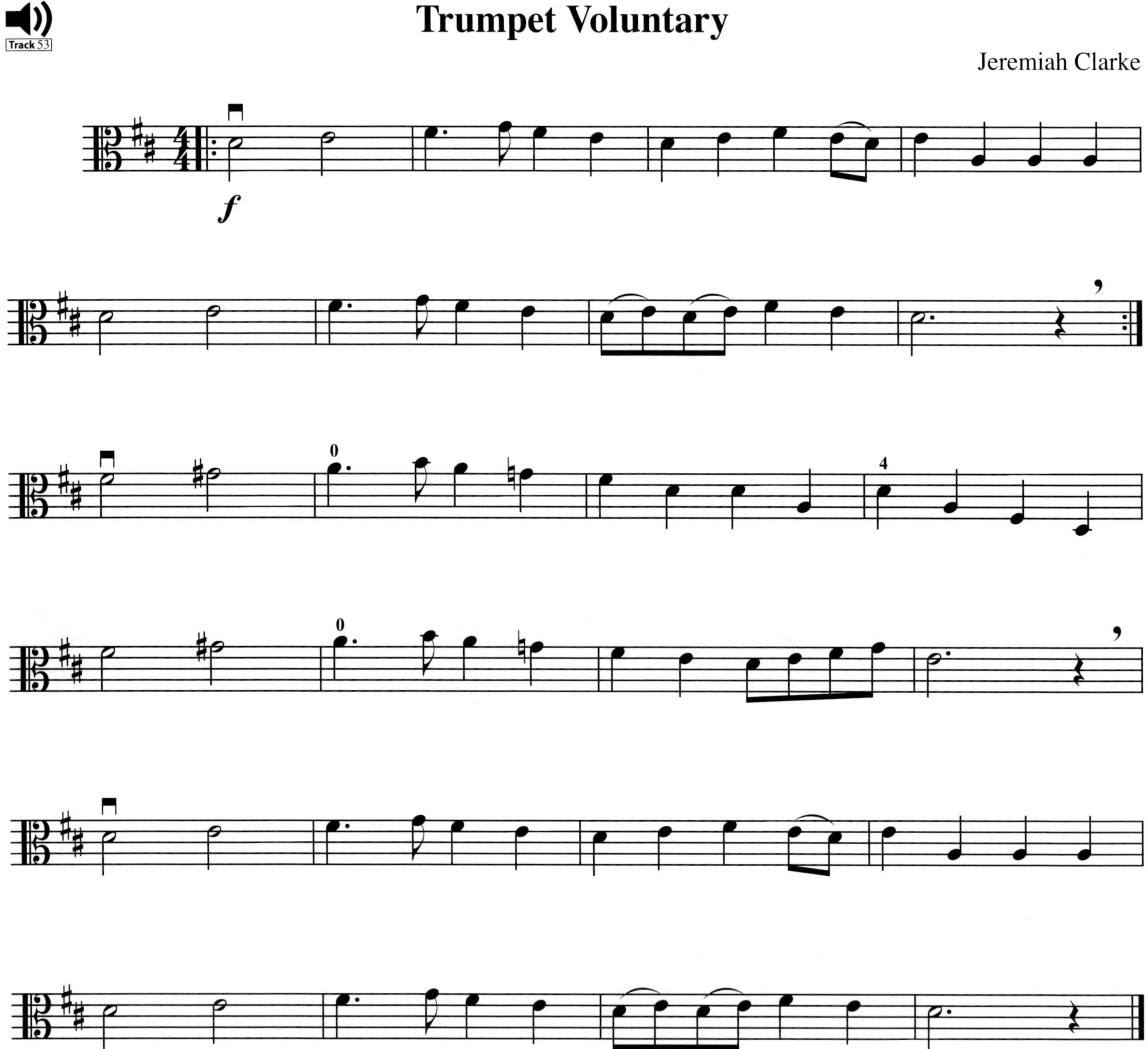

Lesson 21

Sixteenth Notes

A **sixteenth note** is worth half of an eighth note, and there are four sixteenth notes in a quarter note. A single sixteenth note has two flags, and multiple sixteenth notes are usually connected by a double line.

Track 54

Light Cavalry Overture

Franz von Suppé

Track 55

Sleepers Awake

J. S. Bach

Lesson 22

First and Second Endings

When a piece of music has a repeated section that changes slightly at the end of the second time it is played, it is written with **first and second endings**. These are marked with a bracket and either the number 1 or 2 over the measures. When playing the music the first time, play through the bracketed first ending to the repeat sign, then go back to the beginning or the previous repeat sign as with a regular repeat. The second time through, skip over the measures of the first ending and proceed to the second ending.

Lesson 23

Accents

An **accent** means to play a note with extra emphasis. It is written in music as a wedge symbol above a note. Apply slight pressure to the bow with the right index finger in order to produce a sharp, heavy beginning to the note.

Lesson 24

Dotted Eighth Notes

A **dotted eighth note** is worth one and a half eighth notes, or three sixteenth notes.

Lesson 25

Tempo

Tempo refers to the speed of a piece of music. Tempo markings appear at the beginning of a piece. Some examples of different tempo markings are:

Slow: *Lento, Largo, Adagio* Moderate: *Andante, Moderato* Fast: *Allegro, Vivace, Presto*

Lesson 26

Ritard

The word **ritard** means to slow down and often appears at the end of a piece of music. It is sometimes abbreviated *rit*.

Intermezzo

Pietro Mascagni